I Will Rise

An Autobiography of
a Successful Entrepreneur

ROCHENEL MARC

I WILL RISE: An Autobiography of a Successful Entrepreneur.

Copyright © 2018 by Rochenel Marc.

All rights reserved. Printed in the United States of America. No part of this book may be used or reproduced in any manner whatsoever without written permission, except in the case of brief quotations embodied in critical articles or reviews.

Unless otherwise indicated, all Scripture quotations are taken from the King James (American Version).

Editor & Publisher:

www.hcpbookpublishing.com

Book and Cover design by HCP Book Publishers

ISBN: 978-1-949343-05-2 (paperback)

ISBN: 978-1-949343-06-9 (eBook)

First Edition: July 2018

Table of Contents

Dedication v
Acknowledgments vii
Preface xi

Chapter 1
Humble Beginnings 1

Chapter 2
Learning Years 7

Chapter 3
Tough Choices 17

Chapter 4
Transitioning 25

Chapter 5
The Best Years of My Life 33

Chapter 6
Embracing Entrepreneurship: The Path to Success 47

Chapter 7
What I Have Learned 53

Epilogue
Picturesque Journey 61

Dedication

I want to dedicate this book to my wife, my best friend, Maudeline Marc, who is always by my side no matter what, for better and for worse. When I was on the verge of giving up, she said, *"Marc, don't let anything stop your dream. You can do it!"*

This book is also dedicated to my children. Never take anything for granted. If I can do it, you can do it too, but you must play by the rules. Demonstrate love and respect for others and stay in school. You have a greater opportunity for education in the United States of America than in any other country, so make use of it.

Finally, I dedicate this book to my sister, Jolene, who brought me to the land of opportunities.

Acknowledgments

I want to acknowledge some key people who play an important role in my life, who have helped me achieve many goals, and contributed to making this book a success. They have encouraged me, especially when my self-esteem was low.

To my wife and best friend, Maudeline Marc. Thank you for never giving up on me, for your continued support and encouragement when it is needed the most.

To my daughter, Natasha, who always encouraged me throughout my school years. She always says, *"Dad, I am proud of you. You have inspired me."* After graduating with my Master's degree, she said, *"Dad, I need to work harder to get my PhD. I want to go above you."* You are truly an inspiration. Thank you.

To Dr. Michelle, my social worker, and professor while I did my undergraduate studies at Barry University.

To the rest of my graduate professors, thank you for pushing me beyond my perceived limitations.

To my friends and advisers, Jonathan Fried, Marie Flore, Fritz Philogene, Shanel Sylvain, Willio Charles, Gerald

Mercilien, Marie Maude Ketant, Marie C. Andre, Rev. Anthony Martin and his wife, Sister Henriette Martin, Bishop Johannes Bazelais, Elizabelle Delva, Marie Franguel, Alpha Fleurimond, and Pierre Clark, thank you all for your consistent encouragement.

To Rev. D.C., my friend, and adviser, who helped me choose the title for this book.

To my nieces, Carline Andre, Ella Marc, Nadeige Andre Mylande A. Desir, and Diana Marc, thank you.

To my academic advisor from Barry University, Sylvia Perra, and Miss Patricia Cook, thank you.

*I Am Not a Failure;
My Success Was Just Delayed.*

~ R. Marc

*To those from a humble beginning
who are presently navigating the treacherous
waters of life, know that success delayed
is not success denied.*

~ R. Marc

Preface

One thing I don't like is when people feel sorry for me. I always take responsibility for my own actions. When you feel sorry for me, I feel guilty. With that said, I am not sharing my autobiography with the world to get pity points. I want to send a message that it doesn't matter who you are, or where you are, you can achieve success with hard work and a healthy dose of determination. I want to inspire someone to not give up, but to keep trying until the silver lining in your dark cloud reveals itself.

I have had a very hard life so far. I was not planning to write an autobiography and had even helped other classmates write about me. In my final month of undergrad studies at Barry University, I began to slowly change my mind. Professors told me that this was something I needed to do, and I should not ignore the inclination to inspire others through my tale. Friends and classmates encouraged me to do it, but I was still hesitant until my wife, Maudeline, said, *"Marc, stop being afraid. You can do it."* She said I owed the world that much, and it was more for my children and the people who contributed to who I am today.

I contacted a ghostwriter/publisher in early 2017, and it was not until 2018 before I actually began the process. It's a long time coming, but I have a story to tell in recognition of others who may be traveling the same road that I am more than familiar with. If you have been through what I have been through, then this is for you.

Maudeline said, *"Go ahead and do it."* She's my greatest cheerleader and a source of strength and inspiration in my life, so I decided to put my story together and make this project a reality. This is a personal memoir; it is not a definitive history of the major events that happened in my life, which I was privileged to take part in. We can never tell the whole story because others may be implicated in the process, but I can share enough to give a weary heart hope.

I hope this short biography will prove useful to my children, friends, and many other immigrants who came to the land of opportunity (United States of America) but lost the opportunity for a better education by making excuses instead of persevering through the rough waters. I could have made excuses too but chose not to. I left my family behind to migrate to a foreign country. I left my mother and sisters, and it wasn't an easy thing to do, but the end does justify the means. I can look back today with very little regret because everyone is better off now because of the sacrifice I made then, and my determination to succeed.

This is my story, and it is a story about hard work, determination, sacrifice, and playing by the rules. I have had a rough time in my life. This is a story about people who helped me become who I am today. Your success is not dependent on where you come from, the color of your skin, or your nationality. Success comes through self-determination and recognizing the path that will take you from one place to another to improve your lifestyle on a daily basis.

I faced many problems along my journey, as many of you are facing now. Some I will share, others will remain in my heart to ponder. Maybe there will be other more revealing volumes in the future. I want you to know what I have been through, where I am coming from, and where I am today. I don't necessarily want to tell my story in a linear fashion, because my life feels kind of disjointed. So I may jump back and forth between years and incidents but still try to be clear. As I process my thoughts, the memories come back, so if you find me being repetitive, pay close attention because something new will be revealed in the process.

Finally, don't be offended by my story. It is not my intention to offend anyone, but it can be a challenge to share one's testimony without speaking bluntly about certain things. I carry no ill feelings for anyone who has passed through my life, good or bad, and I genuinely wish everyone well. So let's get to it.

CHAPTER 1

Humble Beginnings

I was born and raised in a small town in Haiti called *Elvina*. It was not only small, but it lacked the necessities of community life. There was no running water, no electricity, no toilet, no access to public transportation, and no public or private schools.

I was born on January 1, 1967. The population of Elvina was estimated to be an average of about thirty-five people, which included friends, neighbors, and family members. Elvina was located in the mountains, on the north-west side of Haiti, in the country area.

My parents had eight children—four boys and four girls. I am the last of all my siblings and the one more prone to be preyed upon. It is strange how we can be born into the poorest of circumstances yet think we are normal until we start comparing ourselves to others. We thought our lives were normal, though we lacked so many things.

My mother, Isenara, and my father, Poncius, were both born and raised in the Catholic Church, but they believed in voodoo witchcraft. Their marriage did not last. My father had seven brothers and three sisters. My mother had four brothers, and she was the only girl in the family. All my dad's brothers were married, had children, and lived in the same neighborhood as a family tradition. My mom's family lived far, about fifty kilometers away.

My father was a farmer. He grew crops for a living, and he was the only one who had the opportunity to go to school. He later became a priest, or what we called "Pere Savan" in Haiti.

My mother worked as a day laborer with the local middle-class people who owned big farms. She was never given the opportunity to go to school, but she managed to raise eight children with no government help.

My father left my mom when I was three months old. They were never divorced, just separated. It was a very difficult time for our family. I was the last child, so it really impacted my life; it impacted everybody's life. It was a time of confusion and emotional turmoil. Somewhere between 1970 and 1975, my mom was diagnosed with depression and anxiety.

When I was seven years old, my dad came back for the first time and took me away from my mother. He took me to a stranger's house, where I was forced to labor as a houseboy. I served that house as best as I could. I had an itinerary of things to do that included washing dishes, cleaning the house, taking care of the cows and goats, and any other labor work required. I lived with that stranger for approximately three years. During that time, I was emotionally and psychologically abused. I was cursed and called all kinds of names for no apparent reason. It was constant and overbearing, and I had no idea how to process what had become of my life. I had no idea how to communicate with my mom, or my brothers and sisters until she found out about what my dad took me away to do. She then ensured that I returned home.

The psychological onslaught did not cease. My cousin on my father's side, who is still alive but not doing well financially, consistently told me I would never amount to anything. I heard this statement many times for many years to come, but I knew I could be better. I knew somehow that I had to be tough and keep my focus because I believed anyone could succeed if they had the opportunity to go to school and if they also worked very hard. I learned hard work from Mom. She taught us to use our minds and hands to get what we want, and not to steal.

I found that the older we get, after enduring much verbal abuse as children, the harder it is to silence that little nagging voice in the back of our heads that would try to remind us we are nothing and would amount to nothing. It takes great determination to push through all that mess, and I learned very early that I was stronger than I thought. I endured enough trauma in my life to break me and push me beyond the limits of sanity, but I never lost my mind. It is that inner strength that propelled me along.

CHAPTER 2

Learning Years

I returned home to my Mom at the age of ten, one week before my birthday. My mom enrolled me in a public school, and I had to walk one and a half hours to and from school every day.

There was no money, so many times I had to go to school without the means to purchase anything. I would go to school hungry because Mom didn't have enough to feed me in the morning.

The public-school system used to provide lunches for students who were deprived or in need. I was more than deprived—I was stressed, depressed, filled with anger, and suffering from anxiety. Furthermore, my three years' experience as a houseboy took a mental toll on me because I was treated like a slave. They consistently yelled at me and called me names. I was never physically abused though, but sometimes it's hard to determine which is worst—verbal or physical abuse. I have no preference for either, but for a young mind, that environment had adverse effects on shaping my personality.

I started school with one pair of pants and a worn shirt. Mom couldn't afford new clothes. What shocked some people was that, despite my lack, I was one of the smartest kids in my class. I understood the importance of education and knew that if I got the opportunity, I would not take it for granted.

In 1982, I graduated from middle school with honors. I worked harder than anyone else around me because I needed to prove to myself, and the naysayers in my family, that I was not dumb. I could make something of myself; I just needed the right opportunities. While the glory of that moment was short-lived, I basked in the moment of grandeur and success I experienced, the thrill and satisfaction of hearing my name called on the honor roll. I savored the taste of triumph in that moment, and I knew I wanted to experience that feeling again and again.

However, after middle school, I realized I wouldn't be able to go any further due to financial constraints, so I decided to quit school. Mom was experiencing financial hardship unlike anything we had been through before. She didn't have any support, and she was not able to continue to push any further. I had to quit school and find something else to do.

Later in the year, I decided to go to a tailoring school in the neighborhood, but it wasn't the best choice for me. After nine months, I quit. Then I started doing agriculture work to help my mom financially. During the summer, I also tutored about fifteen neighborhood kids for little money. That was my first experience tutoring students, and I remember enjoying it. The thing about having an innate ability is that at some point in your life, you will get an opportunity to taste it through experience. You will see how this became a significant part of my life later in the story.

My mom owned a piece of property in a rural part of Haiti. In 1984, she sold it to send my sister, Jolene, to the United States of America. That piece of land was the only source of wealth for the family in case of an emergency or someone in the family died. It was the only way we could afford anyone's funeral expenses. Mom sold it and paved the way for Jolene to go to the States. This was a blessing for us, but Jolene had to do all kinds of tasks to help us financially. She is a caring person, so finding odd jobs that the American citizens did not want was not difficult. Today, I am grateful to Jolene who played a key role in helping me achieve my education and success.

So Jolene migrated and took care of the family for two years, then she brought me to the states. The necessary arrangements were made, and, in 1986, I traveled by boat to the shores of the famed United States. I spent five days in the high sea afraid I would not make it. I knew the stories. Many of my people perished at sea trying to cross the ocean to a better life. They never made it. One Thursday at 3:30 a.m., I found myself on the shores of South Florida.

I left home with two pairs of pants, two shirts, and no money. I came to a country where I didn't speak the language. It was a tough time, and I found it hard to cope with the system, the culture, and the food.

Like most Haitians, I always dreamed of going to America one day to see how beautiful this county was. Again, we heard the stories. I always thought everything was free in America. What a culture shock I experienced when I got here. I also thought white people were always giving away free stuff or money. How ignorant can one be? It took me a few months, but once I realize how far from reality my thinking was, I knew I had to lay aside the fantasies and change my view about this country. I had expected to find money growing on trees, easily accessible to the common man, but that was not the reality I now faced.

I have always been very observant and flexible enough to adapt to any circumstance. I learned quickly that you can be whatever you want to be, but you must play by the rules. You cannot change the system, but if you want to benefit from it, you must adhere to the established rules. I worked seven days a week. My jobs over time involved picking beans, tomatoes, strawberry, and bell peppers; cutting grass; working the nursery; landscaping; dishwashing; and cooking. Yes, I wore many hats, and I am not ashamed of it. I was earning an honest living and could do more for my family financially, but I still wanted more. I understood the new country of which I was now a part. To move up the ranks, I needed to increase my education. I would not be able to do that unless I could speak their language. So in 1989, I started going to night school to learn English as a second language.

I often reminisced about my life's journey. I respected my mom for working menial tasks to get us by. I honor her for sacrificing the only asset we owned as a family to make a way for us to better ourselves. It worked because we had ambition. We were determined that poverty would not be our lot, and we were willing to make the necessary sacrifices to ensure that we pulled through. It was a tough call, but if you know us now, you would agree that all the trauma and hell we went through was worth it after all.

One reason, if not the main reason, Mom never received a formal education was that it wasn't a priority for girls to go to school in those days. Women were always classed as the weaker vessel, but if we really think about it, where would we be without their resilience? I learned the importance and value of many things because we lacked them, and I wasn't about to take for granted any opportunity that presented itself, that allowed me to go higher than anyone else in my family.

Jolene going to the United States was a blessing. It opened the door for me to follow and provided the opportunity I so desperately needed. While my journey was not a pleasant one, I was not among the statistics of those who traveled by boat and did not make it.

For seven years, I lived with Jolene, her two children, and her husband. Seven years is a long time to live at somebody's place, but I needed time to get my feet on the ground. I wasn't prepared for the many experiences life was about to throw my way, but I am happy that I had a proper foundation on which to stand and family who had my back most of the time.

I was a farm worker for the better part of the first three years in the United States. I took all the jobs that the citizens of this great country scoffed at. It was hard work and long hours, but it provided financial stability, which I needed above everything else. During that time, I learned a lot. I became the jack of all trades and master of all.

Then came October 1992 and Hurricane Andrew. The hurricane had hit hard and, in the aftermath, I lost everything. My brother-in-law was covered by the insurance company but he didn't want to assist me from what he collected, so they put me out of the house. My sister said nothing in my defense. I understand his reason; he didn't want the word to get out in the community that he had collected insurance money. I remember it was a Sunday afternoon. I was just coming in from church, and someone was waiting for me at the front gate. The individual told me I was not welcomed at that house anymore, and I needed to get out. At the time, I was driving a blue 1980 Nissan B2010. I had to beg the individual to give me a chance to get my stuff from the house. They allowed me to go inside. I packed my clothes and other small items and hit the road, not even knowing where I was going, with tears in my eyes.

While I was driving in the neighborhood, I saw a For Rent sign near a bush. I knocked on the door. A short Hispanic-looking old man with grey hair came out asking if he could help. I explained that I was looking for a place to stay. I rented the place for $250 a month.

It was a run-down house, and I was afraid to sleep at nights because I was afraid snakes might bite me. I will continue this story in the next chapter.

I remember one person who was always there for me no matter what. His name is Gerald. I called him Father Sauveur. He moved in with me and stayed with me until my first wife migrated to the United States and moved in. He was a good friend.

So, I knew what it felt like to be homeless, even if it was only for a short time. Throughout all that, I still have a good relationship to this day with my brother-in-law. It's pointless to keep offense in the heart because it can make you sick. I wanted to live my life free from harboring negative thoughts and feelings for anyone. We all do what we think we need to do for the betterment of our own lives, and the families we are responsible for. Sometimes we judge other people for the decisions they make, but if we found ourselves in a similar position, we would probably make the same choice.

I found myself homeless, with nowhere to go and no one to turn to, and I had nothing because the storm took everything. But the day I had to leave my sister's house was one I will never forget because I believe it was a turning point in my life. During that time, I was working as a dishwasher and a cook at a local restaurant. I was also attending night school for a couple of years, so my finances were somewhat depleted. I was just learning to speak the Queen's language, so I was in quite a predicament. That Sunday afternoon I found myself empty and homeless, which was weird initially because my family always stuck together. I knew I had to find a resolve within that I hoped was there. That incident forced me to push and work harder than I ever have in my life. It also provoked me to take my education seriously.

Bad things happen in our lives, not necessarily because people are trying to destroy us, but it eventually serves a purpose to push us to a higher place. Every single incident in my life that was labeled bad helped me somehow. I think our success depends on how we perceive life. It is the half-glass full or half-glass empty perception at work every day, and our perception will determine many of the outcomes in our lives.

CHAPTER 3

Tough Choices

After losing everything to Hurricane Andrew and finding myself homeless with nowhere to go and no one to turn to, I accepted Jesus in my life. I got baptized in a Baptist church, the same church I attend today. As I mentioned before, I was raised in the Catholic church, because that was the religious culture my parents knew, but I felt I needed a little more than recital prayers and rituals. I needed to find and know God on a personal level because I needed Him more than I have ever needed anyone during that time. I needed to know He was real. That was a season of tough choices for me. It was up to me to decide which direction my life was going, and I needed additional assistance.

My family was not happy about my surrendering to Jesus. Everyone was Catholic, and they believed in voodoo, so they didn't even want to hear the word 'Christian.' I wanted to break out of the norm, transcend family tradition to embrace something new, and I wasn't about to let anyone deter me. The people around me believed that voodoo would solve their problems. I admit it does produce some results, but I wanted to embrace a higher power, so I turned to Jesus. The moment I did that, my life changed. I have no regrets because following Jesus has made me a better person. I learned to act and think differently, using my common sense a bit more. I learned to forgive those who treated me badly, and I could forgive quickly. I learned not to harbor offense in my heart but to let it go. I believe God is King, and I am a prince in His courts, and I don't take the life I live for Him lightly.

Becoming a Christian also brought some unwarranted opposition from co-workers and friends, in addition to family members. They viewed church as a money magnet, a place where the poor are depleted of all their money to make a pastor rich. I don't believe that is true, even though there are exceptions. I refused to allow anything to turn me back from the course I had chosen, and I have held on to my faith in Jesus Christ to this day.

I found myself homeless, so I packed up the few things I could find in the trunk of my car and drove around the neighborhood trying to find somewhere to stay. I didn't think about going to a hotel at the time. My mind was on finding a house, and, as stated before, I did find a small house to rent in the middle of nowhere, in the bushes, with no electricity and no running water. I stayed at that house for three days. The rent was $250. I moved out three days later after finding another place in a bad neighborhood. I had no idea what I was getting myself into. At night, there was incessant knocking at the door from people trying to sell me drugs. There was a lot of gun violence and prostitution, and I found it difficult to sleep at night. I still managed to stay at that place for three months before I was able to move into a better neighborhood.

In March 1990, I returned to Haiti and met my first wife. We had grown up in the same neighborhood and gone to school together. It was easy to establish a connection and relationship based on that. All our friends in the neighborhood were getting married, so, of course, we wanted to get married too. Call it an emotional decision, but one year later, we got married. I hadn't planned for marriage, so the beginning of our marriage was a little shaky. I sometimes think I rushed into marriage because I was not properly educated. Having a job, going to school, and taking care of a wife and children was a huge responsibility I wasn't fully prepared for. To complicate matters even worse, I went back to the United States and left my wife and young child in Haiti. I had intended to get the paperwork done so she could come up soon, but, for some reason, it took years.

I continued to work and pursue my education, and when I got a chance, I went to Haiti to be with my wife. It was a tough decision to live with. I always considered myself a smart young man, but there were times I knew I didn't think certain things through.

In 1992, my wife gave birth to a baby boy. He was just like me, and I loved him. His name was Marvens. Unfortunately, his young life was cut short because of neglect. One day, his mother was away from home, and Marvens was asleep inside the house. The maid went to buy goods at the market. When she came back, the house was on fire. My son died in the fire. All they found was his charred bones.

I often think that if Haiti was as developed as the United States of America, my son's life would have been spared because the resources needed within the community to prevent such a tragedy would have been in place, for example, fire rescue. Haiti lacks certain resources, especially in some of the poorer communities. We didn't have access to a lot of things, to our own detriment. I also feel that the Haitian government should put laws in place that would protect children against child neglect. It happens too often, and the perpetrators usually get off without being held accountable or facing any consequence. Someone should have been held responsible for the death of my son, but, unfortunately, no one was. That has left me traumatized to this day, especially when I see children who would be the same age as him. I often cry at such sightings.

In all I have been through, I consider myself like Job of the Bible. When he lost his wife, children, and all his wealth, he still maintained his integrity and hung on to his faith in God.

After the death of my son, I became more focused on my profession and education. It took me several years to recover somewhat from what was now in the past and be more focused on my future. In August 1995, I graduated as an Automotive Technician from the Robert Morgan Vocational Technical School. That was a momentous occasion, as I was now gradually seeing the fulfillment of my dreams, and the result of my years of hard work.

In 1995, I started to work as a mechanic. I held that position for almost nine years. In 1996, I attended the Miami Dade College while I was working for Sears Automotive as an alignment technician.

In June 1998, I was finally able to complete the application process so my wife could come to the States. I brought her and our older daughter over in 1999. Our second daughter was born in October of that same year. We divorced six months later because she was unfaithful while living in Haiti. I do blame myself for choosing to have a long-distance relationship, but again, I didn't think through my decision to get married, so it was always a trying period for us both. She even confessed to being unfaithful on more than one occasion, and that tore me apart. I knew I couldn't continue in the marriage any longer, so we dissolved it.

Marriage is a long-term commitment, and we take the vows we make before man and God too lightly. We vowed *"for better or for worse, in sickness and in health,"* but very often we really don't mean it. I tried my best to glean every lesson I could from my first marriage because I didn't want to make the same mistake again. If I got married a second time, I wanted to be serious about our vows.

Not long after my divorce, I started dating someone I had known for over twenty years. She was also a divorcee, like me, so we connected on another level. We started dating in 2002, and a year and a half later, we were married. I had fallen in love with her, but again, I think we made a hasty decision. We overlooked some very important things, thinking we could handle it as adults, with experience. We were wrong. It was another bad choice in my life. That marriage lasted for only four years.

I graduated from Miami Dade in 2003 with a degree in Human Resources. In the summer of 2007, I divorced my second wife. Her family did not agree with us getting married. Her mother thought I was too poor for her daughter, and the perception the family had of me put a strain on our marriage, so again, we decided to go our separate ways because it was not working out in our favor.

Never forget that getting married also means we are marrying into a family. It is difficult when the family of the one you love dislikes you for any reason.

My life has been a series of tough choices. I sometimes think we complicate our own lives by the choices we make. I experienced the trauma of losing a child tragically because of my choice to get married quickly, without proper planning and thought. Could I have avoided that trauma by making a different choice? Were the two years I got with my son worth making a bad choice?

We make decisions that cannot be undone, so it becomes pertinent to carefully consider each choice before making it. We have the power to choose, and no power can override the human will.

CHAPTER 4

Transitioning

After my second divorce, I experienced humiliation and rejection from society, family, friends, and, to some extent, the church. I had been a member of that church for many years, and I still am today. I find that it is easy for people to relate to you once you fall in line with their perception of how your life should be lived. It is easy to judge someone from the sidelines, but unless you walk in their shoes, you really can't relate to what the person is going through. All of us are guilty of giving advice we were unable to adhere to once we find ourselves in a similar position.

In Haitian culture, it is not okay to file for a divorce. They don't believe divorcing a spouse is optional, because the vows taken at the altar should be regarded with seriousness and as a lifelong commitment. I do believe that, but not all marriages were meant to last. When two people find themselves in a tense relationship, other alternatives must be considered. It is hard to advise people to stay in a marriage, to their own detriment, especially when we absolve ourselves of any responsibility or accountability in case something tragic happens.

Marriage is highly regarded as a sacred and permanent institution by Haitians, and they frown upon anyone who walks away from their marriage for any reason.

I walked away from two, so my punishment was even more severe. Even if you have a justifiable reason, for example, your life or the life of someone else at risk, or infidelity, it's still not a good enough reason for divorce. So I became somewhat of an outcast. Most of the people around me thought I should have stayed in my marriage, even if it wasn't working out or it was falling apart at the seams. It's kind of a dying to self that makes it easy to be accepted by those around you, but, I just couldn't do it. I could not look beyond our immediate unresolved problems to stay in a destructive marriage.

I have often questioned why we hang on to certain traditions at the expense of another's life and happiness. Why should anyone stay in a marriage when they are verbally and physically abused? Why should one party stay and suffer in a marriage when it's obvious they don't belong together? You are faced with a choice when a broken marriage becomes your reality. Society would love to embrace you and boast about how you have been married for twenty, maybe thirty years, but they seldom celebrate those who find liberty in divorce. The choice comes down to how much you value your own happiness. I have a different view from my peers on this issue because my experience was different and very real. I believe God. I know He hates divorce, according to the Scriptures. We get to live our lives once, and some mistakes must be corrected to be able to move on to something else. It's not easy committing to a relationship. Dreaming about having someone to call our own and living it as a reality is a completely different thing. Marriage demands sacrifice and giving up some of your rights. It's understanding that communication is key and compromise is not optional. It took me a while to learn these lessons.

My second divorce was painful. I decided to focus more on my education and try to live my life without the added pressure of attempting to please everyone. By the way, it is impossible to please everybody and pointless and a total waste of time to try.

In 2004, I started attending Barry University to pursue a bachelor's degree, with a major in Liberal Studies and specializing in Social Welfare. I have always wanted to build a career on helping people. That is where my true passion has always been. I got a job that same year as a Community Organizer for the Haitian and the Latino community. My job description was to focus on workers' rights, immigration, providing school lunch, and cleaning bathrooms. I also participated in a school walk-out to support immigration reform for 13.6 million documented immigrants who live in the shadows in the United States.

In 2005, I was privileged to meet with President George W. Bush, along with some elected officials to discuss immigration reform. I also participated in the rally to return President Jean Bertrand to Haiti in 2004, after the coup d'état led by the U.S., Canada, and the French. For those who don't know what that is, the Wikipedia archives define it as follows:

Coup is when a country or a team attempts *at taking something that is not theirs. The phrase* **coup d'état** *is French, literally meaning a "stroke of state" or "blow against the state." In French, the word "État" (French: [eta]), denoting a sovereign political entity, is capitalized.*[1]

Between 2004 and July 2008, I traveled around the country to advocate for worker's rights, health care, better quality education for my community, and wage theft for those working in the hotel industry in the Florida Keys. I used time on a radio talk show to educate the community about their rights in this country. I also taught adult literacy for two years. That was the most fulfilling job I have ever had in my life. No other passion compares to teaching people how to read and write.

---

[1] https://en.wikipedia.org/wiki/Coup_d%27%C3%A9tat

In 2004, I also met with Governor Jeb Bush in Tallahassee to discuss a possible Temporary Protective Status (TPS) for Haitians who were living in the United States after hurricane Jeanne, which killed over 250 thousand people in Gonaives.

It seemed all was going well for me, but it was never easy. I was living in the country of opportunities, yet I had to work hard to achieve my goals. My experiences have aided me in my career. I know what it means to start from rock bottom and work my way up. I know what it is to do menial tasks and work hard at jobs that the ordinary ambitious people do not want. I have been hopeless and homeless, with no one to turn to. I have experienced broken relationships that I have had to walk away from, painfully.

After the difficulty and trauma of going through two divorces, I realized that both my exes had malicious thoughts toward me. I believed they wanted me to become homeless and an outcast in society. Their hope was to see me sleeping under a bridge or in the streets, begging for food. Maybe if God's hand was not in my life, that is exactly where I would have ended up. But God was for me, so who could be against me? I managed somehow to make it, even though it was a constant struggle for the most part.

There is a Haitian proverb that says, *"What you wish for your mother-in-law, will turn and hunt your mother!"*

I am not sure if that proverb applied to me, but I know that the pain of divorce and rejection was nothing compared to what I experienced on May 11, 2006. I lost my mother on that day. She was the most important person in my life at the time. No matter what I was going through, my mom always planted seeds of encouragement in my life. I was dealing with divorce, child support, and a lot of family drama, so losing her was a heavy blow that I thought I might not recover from.

I went to Haiti to assist with the funeral arrangements and attend the funeral. It was a difficult time for me and my family. We are never really prepared to lose our mother, even when our relationship was nothing to write home about. I was close to my mom, so it took a traumatic toll on my life, and I had to go through that with minor support and still had my own issues to deal with.

When I returned to the United States after burying my mother, my wife had left with our two children. As they say, that was the *'straw that broke the camel's back.'* That led to our divorce the following year and some of the most difficult months in my life. I considered taking my own life. My perception is that family are people who are there for you, especially during difficult times. I lost my family at a time when I needed them the most. During that season, I had never felt more abandoned and rejected in my life.

I knew I was transitioning; I knew I was moving; I knew I was growing, but you don't always get to see where your journey is taking you, and it makes it difficult sometimes. But now I can look back and have a lot of *'Oh'* moments because I see how it all worked together in full harmony to get me where I am now.

> *And we know that all things work together for good to those who love God, to those who are the called according to His purpose. (Romans 8:28)*

CHAPTER 5

The Best Years of My Life

Albert Ellis once said, *"The best years of your life are the ones in which you decide your problems are your own. You do not blame them on your mother, the ecology, or the president. You realize that you control your own destiny."*

We don't get to choose the circumstances we face in our lives, though some of the things we go through are a result of our own choices. But we do have the power to choose how we respond to our circumstances and how we allow them to impact us.

It's hard declaring that I have experienced good years. They were not good in the sense that they were devoid of challenges, or immune to problems, but I learned eventually how to respond to my storms and difficulties differently. It is true that if you change your perception, you can change your life. There are so many books written about this very thing. I will offer some tips gleaned from my own personal research on this topic that may help you change your life today.

I did my undergrad studies at Barry University. It was challenging, but I was focused on getting a good education, so I had to learn to push through the mess in my life. There is no greater teacher than experience. At one point my GPA dropped from 3.0 to 1.5 because of stress and family drama. I thought my life was on a slippery slope to failure, and there was nothing I could do about it. I felt powerless watching my potential slowly diminish into consistent failure. That is where I learned that no man can stand alone and attempting to do so can lead to our demise.

I found a strong support system in my professors at the time, who believed in me and decided they would never write me off. Though some of them were very hard and unfair to me, and others were racists, enough of them believed in me to keep me going. I have mentioned them by name in my acknowledgments.

In 2009, I graduated with my undergrad degree with a 2.92 GPA, and this was while I was working as a security guard. Yes, I managed to raise my GPA, but not because my circumstances had changed. I was still going through a lot, but I had support. I had people in my life who believed in me; therefore, I was encouraged to keep trying and not to give up. It paid off in the end. There is one other person who became a very firm foundation for me in attaining to the success I enjoy today. She is my best friend. I met her two years before I graduated from Barry University.

Maudeline is as beautiful today as the first day I saw her. She quickly became my best friend and greatest fan. She was always standing in the stadium of life cheering me on, telling me I could do it, and encouraging me not to quit. It is no surprise that I made this woman my wife, and the wisest man who ever lived did say that the man who finds a wife finds a good thing. It took me three attempts to get it right, but I did, so the last ten years have been the best years of my life.

We have seen good days, and we have seen bad days, but our life's experience taught us wisdom that allowed us to have a proper, more defined perception of life that caused us to see that the glass was always half full. Our marriage has not been perfect, but it has produced joy for both of us, two boys (ten and three years old at the publishing of this book) and a decade of wonderful memories.

Maudeline migrated to the United States in 2010, after a 7.5 earthquake that ravished the small continent of Haiti, killing almost half a million people. She lost one of her brothers in that disaster, and she is still traumatized today by that event, which is now a major historical reference point in the history of Haiti. From time to time, I have to encourage her heart because of the psychological trauma it caused.

We had met on one of my trips back home. We met on the street where I lived. We became friends before starting a relationship. When we started sharing our good and bad experiences, our hearts connected in such a way that I have never experienced before. She encouraged me to look at life differently and understand that the bad experiences are allowed to teach us to be better people. We laughed, we talked, and we shared tough times and common goals.

I trust her with my life. Her thoughts and actions toward me only confirmed that she was the one for me. All I needed to do was wait, and I eventually found my soul mate. She is very supportive and caring, even in tough times.

When she came to the United States, she was working two jobs to help with our expenses while I was going to school. Communication between us is so easy; it keeps us both on the same page, so there is no animosity or assumptions and misinterpretations that often lead to additional problems in marriage. It amazes me just how effective good communication can be in alleviating conflicts.

In January 2010, I was accepted at the Barry University to do a master's degree in Public Administration. My wife was elated and supported and encouraged me throughout the entire process. It was not easy. The requirements and expectations were high, and the school work overwhelming at times, but I pushed through. It required a lot of focus, time, and sacrifice, but I made it through the three years, and in 2014, I graduated with a 3.4 GPA. I was still working as a security guard and still fulfilling my role as a priest, husband, and father.

The day of my graduation was a memorable milestone for me. No one else in my family had achieved such a feat, and I believe I became an inspiration for many people that they too could achieve what their heart desired.

The Bible teaches us that we can have the desires of our hearts if we delight ourselves in God. I found delight in my walk with the Lord, and I also found satisfaction in achieving my goals and seeing my desires manifest. I had a master's degree. Follow my story carefully and see my humble beginnings, where I am coming from, and you should understand that my life is an example that nothing is impossible for those who believe. It didn't say specifically those who believe in God. If you believe in yourself, you can achieve the impossible.

Now that I had a master's degree, I wanted to find a suitable job that supported my qualifications, but it was not easy because of my age, zip code, and lack of experience. I tried many different avenues to secure a good job but without success. I realized if there was nothing suitable for what I had to offer, I had to create it. This opened me up to pursue a path of business and entrepreneurship. I became more focused on creating my own business. I will talk more about this in the next chapter.

I remember when I had just lost my job, my wife still decided to marry me. I didn't know how I would provide for her and a family, but she trusted me to find a way. That helped push me in the right direction. I knew I couldn't give up or throw in the towel because every choice I made from that point on would affect more than just me. I eventually started working as a security guard.

When my wife arrived in the United States, we could only afford to stay in a one-bedroom apartment, with my son. I was making a good enough salary as a security guard, but we did not see any surplus because I had to pay child support to my two previous wives, and it was a large portion of what I was making. The rest of my salary was used for rent, food, car repair, paying utilities, and helping my family back home in Haiti, so my paycheck at the end of the month was all but depleted.

I remember passing McDonald's one day with my older son in the car. He said he was hungry and asked if I could purchase something for him at McDonald's. Every United States citizen knows McDonald's is one of the most affordable fast-food joints in the country. Almost anyone can afford to buy a meal there. However, that day, I had to disappoint my son because there was not enough money to even buy a Happy Meal. I cried that day because I was unable to afford to provide what my son needed at the time. It's bad when you can't afford to buy anything at McDonald's.

Today, we are not wealthy, but my family can afford to eat whatever they want. That became a goal for me. I wanted to be able to afford life and never disappoint my children again as I did that day. But I knew it wouldn't happen by working for someone else and helping them build their dreams. I needed to build my own, and my wife agreed and supported my decision to start a business. I put my faith in God, and I put my faith to work because I was adamant that my life would change. I had worked too hard and sacrificed too much to settle for mediocrity, and a hand-to-mouth salary. I wanted more. I wanted to give my family whatever their hearts desired.

It is so important to have a healthy perception of life to deal with the setbacks that come our way. Unless we learn to ride over the hurdles of life, it will be difficult to get to the finish line. We may not even see the end of our struggles in sight. I could not have done it alone. My wife was there every step of the way. She learned to cope with the ups and downs of my life, and even when I felt like she wanted to be somewhere else, and with someone else, she reassured me that was not the case. She made a vow, and she meant it, for better and for worse. She stuck with me in the good times, and in the bad, making her a full recipient of all that I am today. She is very smart and very flexible. When she came to the States, she took and passed her board exam to become a nursing assistant. In 2014, she graduated at the top of her class at the Brown Marquis College as a registered nurse. She is an awesome woman, and my success would not have been possible without her.

I also have great respect for Pastor Anthony, who is still my pastor today. His church is truly a community church, and I don't know where I would be today if it wasn't for my church family.

Pastor Constantine is another brother who stood with me in the dark days. He is a true friend, an advisor, and a brother who always provoked me into believing in myself. He made sure I never doubted that I could make it. He placed great value on people and was always ready and willing to help.

These people taught me the greatest lesson I had to learn in life when starting my own business. They taught me that I should love people and give everyone respect. It doesn't matter what their background is, their immigration status, or the color of their skin. Everyone deserves a chance.

What I want you to take from my story is that you can make it, regardless of who you are, where you are coming from, or what you are going through presently. It may just require a shift in your perception, so I want to leave a few tips with you from my own life. Apply them, and you will experience the same results I did.

Albert Einstein said, *"Logic will get you from A to Z, but imagination will get you everywhere."*

Having a wrong perception of life can cause you to experience immeasurable failure. You can be caught in the cycle of doing the same things repeatedly and getting the same results every time. To break free from this cycle, you need to start by doing something different, and that is impossible unless you start to think different.

There was a book written many years ago titled *The Law of Attraction*. I'm sure we have heard of that term. It speaks about the possibility of drawing to yourself the very thing you think about. In other words, you can think things into existence. This is a valuable tool, and we weren't taught the power of imagination growing up. God must have given us that faculty for a reason. So if you are constantly bombarded by a negative outcome, examine your thoughts. It is possible that you are a negative thinker. The good news is, if you are, you can change the way you think. It's not easy, but it is possible. If you don't like the life you are living now, you need to change it. Only you alone can. Don't fall into the trap of thinking everyone around you is the problem. Your perception of life directly affects your life.

So here are some simple things you can apply to your life immediately:

1. Take charge of your life. If you have health issues, lack finances and resources for the basic things in life, have family problems, etc., decide to take charge and be willing to accept responsibility for your actions. Your life is your responsibility, so you should not depend on others to fix it.

2. Set clear goals—long term and short term—and go after them. Add timelines if you need to, but make sure you do something every day toward achieving your goal. People who fail to make goals are the ones who make excuses instead. Don't do that, because you would be setting yourself up for failure.

3. Change the voice within from saying *"I can't"* to *"I can."* You can do anything you set your mind to do. I was a Haitian Native; English was not my language, yet I attained a master's degree in a predominantly English-speaking country. That should tell you something.

4. Use your imagination to see yourself where you want to be. This is where the Law of Attraction begins to work for you. Don't see failure, see success, even if you are failing. Write down what you imagine. This is very powerful, so don't think you are wasting your time. Also, don't dream too small.

5. Refuse to look at what is bad or going wrong in your life. Your power to choose enables you to see only what is good, but you have to choose to look at it. See the good; ignore the bad.

6. Look within yourself and identify everything good about you. Try to understand your strengths and weaknesses. This is important in helping you focus on where your true passion is. There is no benefit in hating yourself or thinking you are worthless and have no value. If you are doing this, you are only digging a hole for yourself. You have more potential than you realize, but maybe you need to stop comparing yourself with others.

7. Finally, don't settle. You may think your current experience is your lot in life, but if you want more, you can get it.

Your perception will become your reality. You will still have bad days, but they will no longer succeed in derailing you from going after your dreams.

CHAPTER 6

Embracing Entrepreneurship: The Path to Success

Growing up, it never crossed my mind that I could run my own business. Even in the initial stages of pursuing my education, I never thought it possible. My goal was to earn a degree and get a good job, with a good boss. When I earned my master's degree, I could not get a job, so I created my own. In September 2010, I founded Nord Ouest Security School, and later I changed the name to South Dade Security School and Learning Center. I was the CEO of my own company.

Before I formed my own company, I was struggling to keep up with child support for both ex-wives. I knew it was mandatory, so I honored my commitment. It meant living within our means and settling for a smaller living space, and less of the amenities of life, but it was always a struggle, and it was something I assumed getting a master's degree could remedy. I never gave the path to entrepreneurship a thought until one day my friend, Pierre Clark, told me that the only way I would survive economically was to start my own business. Clark, thank you for that advice.

My wife was now a registered nurse, working as a CNA, so all we needed was an idea and the resources to get the business off the ground. I had experience as a security guard but recognized I needed training, which didn't exist at the time. When drafted into a company, we had to learn on the job or be trained by those who already understood the demands of the job. I thought it would be a good idea to train students, then release them into the workforce as trained security guards.

When I started my company, many believed it would not succeed. It's the perception of people whenever you attempt anything new. They doubt it will survive because no one else had ever tried it, or maybe all previous attempts had failed. I had a different outlook on life. I knew you could never judge the validity of something by the initial results but persevering through the dross can take us to the other side where we experience success. So persevere I did. When it seemed things were not going as planned; I pressed on. When all the evidence of failure was stacked against me, I pushed through. When everyone was shaking their head in an *"I told you so"* fashion, I ignored the gestures and moved forward.

My first year was tough. I had 65 students that were trained to become security officers. It was a small amount, and we managed to break even financially. I was encouraged enough to go on, though I wasn't sure if it would get any better or if the numbers would increase. After all, just how many young people genuinely wanted to be trained in this field?

In the second year, the numbers almost tripled, and we were ecstatic. We had 160 students in training. By the year 2017, we had over 300 students, and our school was established as the only Security School for the South Dade area. This was a massive accomplishment for my family.

Our business caused a lot of doors to open in a short space of time. We were able to move from our one-bedroom flat, stop paying rent, and bought our first home—a three-bedroom, two-bathroom house. We also bought three other houses in Haiti. We are indeed blessed. When we look back at where came from to where we are today, we must be grateful to God for both giving us the potential to become more than we dreamed we could ever be and providing the means and support to make it all happen. He is no respecter of persons, so what He has done for us, He will also do for you.

I was then able to focus on my true passion, which was becoming an advocate for people who find themselves on a similar road that I had previously walked. I was a voice for those who were not heard, and there are many testimonies out there of the impact we have had on the lives of many of our brothers and sisters. We have helped so many, we lost count.

I became focused on immigrants from Haiti and Latino worker's rights and wage theft. I remember a lady named Fransieuse Fortune. She was from Haiti visiting the United States, and she overstayed on her visa for personal reasons. She had a three-month-old baby. One day, while she was breastfeeding her baby, ICE showed up and detained her and separated her from her baby. I intervened by bringing the community together for a press conference. We met with the Director of Immigration three days after the incident, resulting in her release and reuniting her with her child. She is now an America Citizen.

We all have dreams we want to accomplish. For some, the road is more difficult than others. Most of us weren't born with a gold spoon in our mouth, as the saying goes. We all have to work to achieve whatever goals and dreams we set for ourselves, and even if God gives us a vision, we must put our faith to work in a practical sense to see it come to fruition. Entrepreneurship was my path to success. I don't believe I could have achieved it any other way. I had the qualification but was told that I lacked experience when I sought a good job congruent with my education. I was not deterred by the rejection I received during this time. Instead, I created something new, and I was able to offer good jobs to others as well. I was the employee that became the employer, and it felt good to wear that hat.

My advice to you is to never give up. I believe each of us has at least one business idea within us that is worth exploring. You will either succeed or you will fail, but I think it is worth the risk. The Scriptures say in Deuteronomy 8:18 that it is God who gives us the ability to create wealth. This, I believe, speaks to the core of who we are as human beings. There is something in each of us, and if we can tap into it, we can benefit from it and establish a rich legacy to pass on to future generations.

Don't be afraid to try. People will tell you it won't work, but the success of what you put your hands to does not depend on other people's opinion but on what you believe about yourself and how much you are willing to sacrifice to see your efforts bear fruit. God will help you. Appreciate your support system, no matter how small it may be, and go after your dreams.

CHAPTER 7

What I Have Learned

My life has become a message for others, and a source of inspiration and motivation, particularly for young men. No matter where you are from, how much you are struggling, and what you have been through, always be your best and think positively. Do not forget that your perception of life eventually shapes your reality, and you have the power to change your life and become whoever you want to become. Listen to your heart and follow your dreams with tenacity, persistence, and focus. If you do these things, you will find success.

The potential for success lies within each of us; we just need to learn to tap into that potential, so it is activated and released. One thing for sure that provokes the activation of our purpose within is suffering.

> *For our light affliction, which is but for a moment, is working for us a far more exceeding and eternal weight of glory, while we do not look at the things which are seen, but at the things which are not seen. For the things which are seen are temporary, but the things which are not seen are eternal. (2 Corinthians 4:17-18)*

Don't be shaken by the bad things you endure, because it serves a purpose to bring out the best in you.

I want to share some additional lessons that I learned through my own journey. If you can grasp the truth of these lessons and apply them to your life, you can accelerate your process in finding purpose and success.

The first important lesson is to never give up and always seek higher education. The purpose of education is to take us to another level, and you can't really put a price on that. People are deterred from furthering their education because of the cost, but whatever the cost, I assure you it is worth it. The value of education is not measurable. Education opens many doors of possibilities; it makes you qualified in a certain area and gives you a proper foundation for establishing yourself as a world changer.

Lesson number two is you don't have to be influenced by what other people think of you. I know racism still exists in America. I have heard the stories and have had a few experiences myself. It may not be outwardly spoken, but you can tell when others close doors of opportunity in your face because you have the 'wrong' skin color. Be proud of who you are. Embrace your uniqueness and ignore those who struggle to appreciate the beauty of life, which is really variety.

The third lesson is if you have been physically or verbally abused as a child, it may be hard to overcome, but it is possible. You need to get over your past and not allow it to define who you are. Your greatest self is always in the future and never in the past. While past experiences help shape your life and even your personality, they don't define you. I had no idea the real potential that sat dormant within me. My fullest potential was realized after being tried by fire and pursuing a higher education, and there is still more to me than what I am presently. For example, I am now a published author. This was just a thought, a dream, something I thought was impossible, but you are holding the evidence in your hand right now of what is possible. The strongest among us are those who learned to transmute their failures and shortcomings into success. You can use your weakness as an excuse not to do anything, or as a platform to go higher. You also must learn to use the negative words of others as stepping stones to go higher.

The fourth lesson I want to share is that you must learn to carefully consider decisions before you make them. I got married twice to the wrong person, and there were initial signs that I ignored. Had I considered what I was about to do, I would probably have made a different choice. I am blessed with children from both failed marriages, and I don't think their entrance into this world was a mistake, so even our bad choices can produce wonderful treasures, but they are still bad choices.

The fifth lesson is good things really do come to those who wait. The Prophet Isaiah penned these words:

> *But those who wait on the Lord shall renew their strength; They shall mount up with wings like eagles, they shall run and not be weary, they shall walk and not faint. (Isaiah 40:31)*

God has a plan for your life, and with those plans come proper timing. Nothing happens before its time, unless you make it happen, which usually leads to a bad decision. God promised Abraham a son, but they couldn't wait, and the Israelites are paying for his decision to fulfill God's promise in his own time and strength. The descendants of Ishmael continue to fight against the Israelites to this day. Whatever God has reserved for you, He only requires that you wait for the time to be right.

Lesson number six is nothing is impossible to those who believe. Those were Jesus' words:

> *Jesus said to him, "If you can believe, all things are possible to him who believes." (Mark 9:23)*

There is an interesting story in the Old Testament about the tower of Babel. All the people on earth spoke one language, and they came together to do something impossible; they were going to build a tower that reached into heaven. The Bible says God came down to see what they were doing. God's response was profound:

> *Indeed the people are one and they all have one language, and this is what they begin to do; now nothing that they propose to do will be withheld from them. (Genesis 11:6)*

No one knows humanity better than He who created us. He knows our true potential, and I believe it is revealed in this story, because some translations say whatever we put our minds to, we can achieve, and nothing will be impossible. That is my greatest lesson in life because I have achieved the impossible because I believed in myself.

As you go forward, maybe there is a business idea you want to pursue or a dream you may have placed on the back burner for far too long. You can do it. So I charge you to love people and give everyone respect—it doesn't matter what their background is, their immigration status, or the color of their skin. We are all on this journey together, though your story will be different from mine. I wish you success, but, above all, I declare over you that:

> *The Lord your God will make you abound in all the work of your hand, in the fruit of your body, in the increase of your livestock, and in the produce of your land for good. For the Lord will again rejoice over you for good as He rejoiced over your fathers, if you obey the voice of the Lord your God, to keep His commandments and His statutes which are written in this Book of the Law, and if you turn to the Lord your God with all your heart and with all your soul. (Deuteronomy 30:9-10)*

EPILOGUE:

Picturesque Journey

In 1995, I was working as a Technician at Sears Auto Center.

Epilogue: Picturesque Journey

This is during my days as a cook.

In 2003, I graduated from the Miami Dade College with an Associate degree.

EPILOGUE: Picturesque Journey

In 2006, I participated in organizing in Homestead for Comprehensive Immigration as an activist community leader.

In 2006, I was a part of a high school walk-out movement to support 13.5 million undocumented immigrants in the United States. Participating schools included South Dade High School, Homestead Senior, and Robert Morgan High School.

EPILOGUE: PICTURESQUE JOURNEY

This was on May 1, 2006, known as International Labor Day. We called it a Day without Immigrants. For the first time, CNN covered this historical event in the small town of Homestead, Florida. It was the first time the community organization, activists, and religious leaders got together to go out on the streets. More the 10,000 people were there marching for one cause.

In 2007, a Haitian Immigrant woman faced deportation for overstaying on her tourist visa. She got picked up by ICE and was separated from her two-month-old baby, who she was breastfeeding at the time. The mother was held in a board detention center awaiting deportation to Haiti. I was called and was able to get the international media attention by calling several press conferences, radio, and television interviews. After we as a community organization met with the Director of ICE, the next day, the woman was released and reunited with her daughter. Now she is a U.S. Citizen, and she is able to work, go to school, and vote.

EPILOGUE: PICTURESQUE JOURNEY

I was given a grand opportunity to teach at a women's leadership and worker's rights seminar. Most of those women were working in a hotel as housekeepers in the Florida Keys. They were abused by their bosses and supervisors because they didn't know their rights and spoke very little English.

This is a family picture in 2008.

Epilogue: Picturesque Journey

Undergraduate in 2009.

I was among the Graduation Class of 2013 with a master's degree.

Epilogue: Picturesque Journey

I was running for office in 2013.

At my office in 2017

Epilogue: Picturesque Journey

This is by no means the end of my journey. I do rejoice today because I am not where I used to be. Hopefully, in five or ten years, I will still be able to make that declaration, because there is still more to do and much to accomplish.

I have seen the fulfillment of many of my short-term goals. One of the goals I have not yet achieved is to meet with the Haitian Government to abolish the suffering of the underaged houseboys and girls who are going through the same thing I was subjected to as a youngster. I want to partner with an organization to help these children go to school. You will read about my accomplishment in these areas in my next book.

Be inspired by my story to never give up on your dreams. Even if you feel like you are at the bottom of the pile, there really is only one way to go, and that's up. Only your efforts, your sacrifice, your perception, and your faith can take you to the top. I will see you there!

www.ingramcontent.com/pod-product-compliance
Lightning Source LLC
Chambersburg PA
CBHW071537080526
44588CB00011B/1697